HEINEMANN STATE STUDIES

New York
Plants and Animals

Mark Stewart

Heinemann Library
Chicago, Illinois

Designed by Heinemann Library
Printed and bound by Lake Book Manufacturing

07 06 05 04 03
10 9 8 7 6 5 4 3 2 1

Library of Congress Cataloging-in-Publication Data
Stewart, Mark, 1960-
  New York plants and animals : New York state studies/ by Mark Stewart.
       p. cm.
Summary: Describes the diverse habitats of New York state and the many animals and plants that live there, including those which are now extinct or endangered.
Includes bibliographical references and index.
  ISBN 1-4034-0356-2 (Hardcover) -- ISBN 1-4034-0578-6 (pbk.)
  1. Natural history--New York (State)--Juvenile literature. 2. Endangered species--New York (State)--Juvenile literature. [1. Natural history--New York (State) 2. Endangered species.] I. Title.
  QH105.N4S75 2003
  508.747--dc21

2002154313

Acknowledgments
The author and publishers are grateful to the following for permission to reproduce copyright material:

Cover photographs by (top, L-R) Donald Specker/Animals Animals, Bill Banaszewski/Visuals Unlimited, Rudi Von Briel/Heinemann Library, Aaron Ferster/Photo Researchers, Inc.; (main) Jeff Lepore/Photo Researchers, Inc.

Title page (L-R) Jeff Lepore/Photo Researchers, Inc., Wendy Neefus/Animals Animals, Robert Lubeck/ Animals Animals; contents page (L-R) A. Rider/ Photo Researchers, Inc., Norman O. Tomalin/Bruce Coleman, Inc.; p. 4 Stephen P. Parker/Photo Researchers, Inc.; p. 5 David Plowden/Photo Researchers, Inc.; p. 6 Winfred Wisniewski/Frank Lane Picture Agency/Corbis; p. 7 Norman O. Tomalin/Bruce Coleman, Inc.; p. 9 Farrell Grehan/ Corbis; pp. 10T, 29, 45 maps.com/Heinemann Library; p. 10B Jeff Lepore/Photo Researchers, Inc.; p. 12 Robert Lubeck/Animals Animals; p. 13T Stephen P. Parker/Photo Researchers, Inc.; pp. 13B, 14B, 15, 28, 44 Bill Banaszewski/Visuals Unlimited; p. 14T Ellan Young/Photo Researchers, Inc.; pp. 16, 22 E. R. Degginger/Animals Animals; p. 17T Jeffrey Stalker/Animals Animals; p. 17B Wendy Neefus/Animals Animals; p. 18 Donald Specker/ Animals Animals; p. 20 S. Callahan/Visuals Unlimited; p. 21 Charles R. Belinky/Photo Researchers, Inc.; p. 23 Carrie Gowran; pp. 24, 25 American Museum of Natural History; p. 26 Mary Evans Picture Library; p. 27T NYSDEC; p. 27B Great Lakes Fishery Commission; p. 30 Ken Lucas/Visuals Unlimited; p. 31 Arthur Morris/Visuals Unlimited; p. 32 Ricardo Azoury/Corbis; p. 33T A. Rider/Photo Researchers, Inc.; p. 33B Leonard Lee Rue III; p. 34 Lynda Richardson/Corbis; p. 37 Aaron Ferster/ Photo Researchers, Inc.; p. 39 Ken Martin/Visuals Unlimited; p. 40 Holt Studios/Nigel Cattlin/Photo Researchers, Inc.; p. 41 Deborah Allen; p. 42 Dick Thomas/Visuals Unlimited; p. 43T Rudi Von Briel/Heinemann Library; p. 43B Marie Read

Photo research by Julie Laffin

The publisher would like to thank Edward H. Knoblauch, M.A., of Syracuse University for his comments in the preparation of this book.

Every effort has been made to contact copyright holders of any material reproduced in this book. Any omissions will be rectified in subsequent printings if notice is given to the publisher.

Some words are shown in bold, **like this.** You can find out what they mean by looking in the glossary.

Contents

New York Habitats

New York state contains roughly 30 million acres of land, ranging from the high peaks of the Adirondacks to the misty shores of the Great Lakes and from the concrete jungle of New York City to the crashing waves on Long Island. On every single acre, some type of plant or animal life exists. In fact, few states can match New York's intense **biodiversity.** Some of the state's **habitats** are untouched by humans; others are human-made. Yet everywhere life persists and evolves and **adapts**—often in remarkable ways.

Many woodland areas in Central New York are filled with beech trees.

Most natural scientists divide New York State into four geographic **ecosystems:** coastal, mountain, plateau, and valley.

Ducks can be found swimming in great numbers in the waters of Suffolk County, Long Island.

New York's coastal ecosystem includes the salt marshes and tidal pools of Long Island and New York Harbor as well as the many freshwater coastal ecosystems that can be found across the state. There are fertile plains and valleys surrounding lakes and rivers. These areas provide an excellent **climate** and soil for growing fruit. The lakes and rivers themselves are the habitat of a variety of fish, plant, insect, and animal life. Coastal areas are important for water birds—particularly ducks and geese—as well as shore birds that **migrate** from the south.

On the North Shore of Long Island is a huge pine **barren.** This area takes up almost ten percent of Long Island's total land surface. It is the habitat of rare **species** of plants and animals such as the **endangered** Eastern tiger sala-mander, the red-shouldered hawk, and the rare dwarf pitch pine tree.

New York's Adirondack and Catskill mountains feature rocky **terrain** and immense forests. Some of the state's most magnificent animals—such as black bear—roam these areas.

Top Twenty Invasive Plants

According to the IPC NY, these twenty plants are the most problematic invasive species in the state:

Black locust
Black swallow-wort
Buckthorn species
Common reed
Curly pondweed
Elaeangnus species
Eurasian water milfoil
Garlic mustard

Honeysuckles (non-native species)
Japanese barberry
Japanese honeysuckle
Japanese knotweed
Japanese stilt grass
Multiflora rose
Norway maple

Oriental bittersweet
Porcelain berry
Purple loosestrife
Spotted or bushy knapweed
Water chestnut

The land stretching west from the Catskills to the shores of Lake Erie is relatively flat and crisscrossed by rivers. This section of the Appalachian Plateau has a huge number of deer.

Finally, the state has fertile plains and valleys surrounding its lakes and rivers. These areas provide excellent **climate** and soil for the growing of fruit.

Something that is continually affecting the balance of these **ecosystems** is the number of invasive plant **species** in the state. Over 30 percent of the plants in New York are not **native** to the state. Invasive plants can destroy **habitats** by crowding out the native plants. With every diminished plant species, animal species within the habitat that feed on those plants can become **threatened** as well. In 1999, the Invasive Plant Council of New York State (IPC NY) was created to work toward

The invasive mustard plant can destroy native grasses and young trees.

The Hudson River and the surrounding area provide an ecosystem for a variety of plants and animals.

minimizing the growth of invasive species in New York and to protect the natural habitats.

The varied habitats of New York all have one thing in common: people. New York's population may soon reach 20 million, and even in the most remote areas the impact of humans has had an effect on the plants and animals there. Some species have **adapted** to humans, while others struggle to survive. This book explores the state's plants and animals, and how the presence of humans helps or hurts dozens of species.

Colonial Living

Believe it or not, the current condition of New York's natural habitats is more like it was in the 1700s than in the 1800s. During the state's rapid growth in the 19th century, large areas of forest were cut down and many streams and lakes were badly polluted. It was not until these areas were cleaned up that many threatened plant and animal species reappeared. Although conflicts between people and nature still exist, today conditions in New York are far better than they were 150 years ago.

New York's Plants and Animals

Spend enough time exploring New York and you will likely spot everything from bald eagles to black bears and whales to wild turkeys. You will find more than 40 **species** of turtles, salamanders, newts, frogs, and small lizards called skinks living in the state and its surrounding waters. Look a little closer, and you will find one of America's best insect populations. New York is also home to many different wildflowers and trees.

MAMMALS

There are nearly 100 **mammals** that make their homes in New York state. Skunks, woodchucks, and opossums forage for food while watching for larger mammal **predators** such as bobcats and bears.

BIRDS

Of course, no single bird can truly represent New York state. When city people think of birds, they are likely to picture pigeons and sparrows. Those living near water are more familiar with geese and gulls.

New York Birds

In all, more than 300 different birds make New York their home for at least part of the year. These include:

- 2 or more types of swans
- 7 kinds of woodpeckers
- 10 types of ducks
- 17 raptors
- more than 20 types of gulls, sparrows, and sandpipers

MARINE LIFE

Wherever you go in New York, you are never far from marine animals. The state's countless lakes, ponds, rivers, streams, and **estuaries**—as well as the Atlantic Ocean—provide **habitats** for hundreds of freshwater and saltwater species. The waters around New York City are full of bluefish and flounder, while off the Atlantic coast swim beautiful sea creatures such as tuna and great white sharks. In the bays of Long Island are millions of clams and oysters, while the lakes in and around New York are home to salmon, sturgeon, walleye, and pike.

PLANTS AND TREES

New York's varied **climates** and habitats are home to an explosion of wildflowers each spring and summer. Sadly, dozens of species are disappearing from the state. They are being **threatened** by humans or by other plants. However, dozens more are doing well, and can be seen in open fields, parks, woodland areas, vacant lots—and even garbage dumps—across the state.

New York state is also a tree lover's paradise. There are more than 18,000 square miles of forest and 150-plus species of trees in the state, including varieties common from the southern United States to the far north of Canada. Trees have played an important role in the state's history and economic development. For thousands of years they provided the wood with which the **native** people built their homes, weapons, tools, and canoes. Later, they were used to build the cabins of early European settlers.

One of New York's wildflowers is the pink lady's slipper. It belongs to the orchid family, and is sometimes used to help relieve tooth pain.

New York Habitats

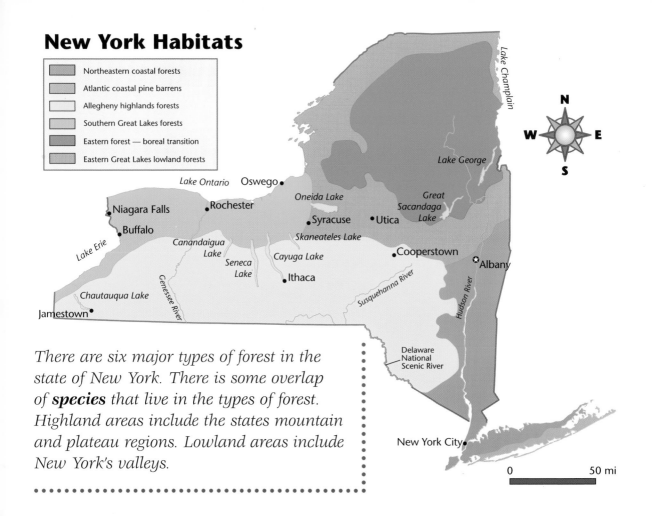

	Northeastern coastal forests
	Atlantic coastal pine barrens
	Allegheny highlands forests
	Southern Great Lakes forests
	Eastern forest — boreal transition
	Eastern Great Lakes lowland forests

Lake Champlain

N
W · E
S

Lake George

Lake Ontario Oswego

Oneida Lake

Great Sacandaga Lake

Niagara Falls Rochester

Syracuse Utica

Buffalo

Lake Erie

Canandaigua Lake

Skaneateles Lake

Cooperstown

Seneca Lake

Cayuga Lake

Albany

Chautauqua Lake

Genessee River

Ithaca

Susquehanna River

Hudson River

Jamestown

Delaware National Scenic River

New York City

0   50 mi

*There are six major types of forest in the state of New York. There is some overlap of **species** that live in the types of forest. Highland areas include the states mountain and plateau regions. Lowland areas include New York's valleys.*

WHITE-TAILED DEER

The most plentiful large **mammal** in New York state is the white-tailed deer. This lively animal has a large tail that is brown on top and white on the bottom and sides. When it runs, it raises its tail, so the last thing you see before it disappears into the **brush** is a bright, white puff of fur.

The white-tailed deer prefers the cover of the woods, but

*With few large **predators** left in New York state, the white-tailed deer's numbers have exploded in many areas.*

Flora and Fauna

Northeastern coastal forests

> flora: sweet gum, Spanish oak, white oak, northern red oak, blue lupine

> fauna: horseshoe crabs, bog turtles, shore birds, loons, Karner blue butterfly

Atlantic coastal pine barrens

> flora: post oak, blackjack oak, pitch pines, maritime grasslands

> fauna: pine **barrens** tree frog, American burying beetles, piping plovers, roseate terns

Allegheny highlands forests

> flora: hemlock, beech, aspen, pin cherry, oak, sedges, grasses, honeysuckles

> fauna: bobcats, black bears, coyotes, flying squirrels, white-tailed deer

Southern Great Lakes forests

> flora: oak, hickory, sugar maple, beech, basswood

> fauna: woodpeckers, screech owls, wild turkeys, green-backed herons, wood thrush, cardinals, white-tailed deer, squirrels

Eastern forest — boreal transition

> flora: balsam fir, black ash, red pine, white pine

> fauna: ducks, moose, black bears, lynx, wolves, snowshoe hares, white-tailed deer, chipmunks

Eastern Great Lakes lowland forests

> flora: eastern hemlock, pines, maples, oaks, white cedar

> fauna: cardinals, downy woodpeckers, wood ducks, eastern screech owls, white-tailed deer, gray squirrels, eastern chipmunks, coyotes, Caspian terns, American bitterns

will **graze** in open meadows if in a large group. Females have one or two young, or fawns, a year, and stand about three feet tall at the shoulder. Males are taller, and have **pronged** antlers. These antlers are used in matches to establish **dominance** over other males and control of a group.

The white-tailed deer prefers to nibble on soft plants, but will eat almost anything if it gets hungry enough. In its search for food, it now comes into regular contact with humans.

BLACK BEAR

The black bear is the most common of the seven bear **species** in the world. The black bear has succeeded because it adjusts well to the changes in its **habitat** brought about by human developments.

Black bears can grow taller than six feet, and can weigh more than 300 pounds. They live about 30 years and prefer to eat fruits, nuts, grasses, herbs, and honey. Black bears have also developed quite a taste for "people" food. More and more, they are leaving the forest and entering campsites and garbage dumps, **endangering** themselves and their human neighbors.

Black bear cubs stay with their mother for two years. By the time they explore on their own, they are strong and knowledgeable in the ways of the woods. If a mother loses her cubs to an accident, she can start a new family almost immediately. In this way, the black bear population is able to recover from any natural or human-made disaster. Although more than 20,000 black bears

The only type of bear in New York state is the black bear.

are hunted in North America each year, their numbers remain very strong.

*Beavers **fell** trees by gnawing at them in an hourglass pattern with their sharp front teeth. They eat the bark and use the wood to build their homes or create **dams** to control the flow of streams.*

BEAVER

The beaver is New York's state **mammal.** It was demand for this animal's, soft, **insulating** pelt that led to the creation of the first trading posts in the state.

Beavers can grow to a length of 3.5 feet and can weigh 60 pounds or more. The beaver's flat, scaly tail once led people to believe it was related to fish, but it is actually a **rodent.** The North American beaver is part of a single species which also lives in parts of Europe and Asia. At one time there were at least 10 different species of beavers in the world.

Beavers live on riverbanks, usually close to soft wood trees such as willow or poplar. The same family often lives for many years in underground lodges or wood-mud-and-rock lodges that can only be reached through an underwater entrance. You know a beaver lodge is nearby when you see a lot of stumps with pointy tops.

Raccoons are easy to recognize because of their black facial "mask" and ringed tail.

RACCOON

Wherever there are trees in New York, you will probably find raccoons. They are skillful climbers and like to nest in tree holes. You will not find them in dry or rocky places, and they also do not like high **elevations.**

A raccoon is always on the prowl. It will rarely sleep in the same place for more than two days in a row.

The male bluebird attracts a female by establishing his territory and building a nest.

Raccoons are **nocturnal.** While they are awake at night, they usually head for the nearest source of water. They look for things to eat like berries, acorns, bugs, or young mice along the way. At the water's edge, they search for eggs, small **rodents,** or baby ducks. They also sink their paws into the mud and feel around for anything **edible.**

BLUEBIRD

The official state bird of New York is the bluebird. Loved for its beautiful **plumage** and sweet song, it is always one of the first **migrating** songbirds to return for spring. There are two types of bluebird in New York—the eastern bluebird and the mountain bluebird—both of which belong to the thrush family of songbirds.

LOON

New York's most unforget-table bird may be the loon. Anyone who has camped at one of New York's **inland** lakes will tell you about its haunting call, which rolls across the moonlit water. New York has two **species** of loon, the common loon and red-throated loon. Loons are big birds, growing to three feet with a wingspan of 50 inches or more. They have large heads, short necks, and straight, strong bills.

Loons live, eat, and sleep almost entirely on the water. They prefer large, deep lakes in forested areas, like in upstate New York. As unforgettable as the sound of a loon is the sight of one taking off. They appear to run across the water, flapping their wings for up to 1000 feet before becoming airborne. They are far more graceful underwater, diving as far as 200 feet in search of food.

Loons have to be fast and flexible swimmers. Not only do they eat fish more than anything else, but large fish sometimes try to make a meal out of them!

This large rainbow trout is swimming near a group of river chubs.

TROUT

The fish for which New York is most famous is the trout. The rainbow trout is the most widespread member of the trout family. It prefers fast-running water, and its silver sides feature a lovely, purplish-red pattern that looks like a rainbow. When rainbow trouts make their way from freshwater to the sea, their markings fade. Then they are known as steelheads. But when they return to their rivers to **spawn,** the rainbows reappear. That is why for many years it was thought that rainbows and steelheads were different **species.**

Rivers of New York that were once filled with brook trout now have a larger population of brown trout. The brook trout were driven away by rising water temperatures—most likely brought on by the cutting down of New York's forests—whereas the brown trout does well in higher water temperatures.

BLACK-EYED SUSAN

Brightening up roadsides, dried fields, and garbage dumps from June through October is the striking black-eyed Susan. A member of the daisy family, it loves open territory. Originally a Canadian wildflower, this large yellow flower with a chocolate-brown center **migrated** south into New York, where it has squeezed out less **hardy** species.

BUTTERCUP

More than a dozen varieties of buttercups bloom in New York state between the months of March and September. The most common is the tall buttercup, which grows in fields and meadows. It has bright yellow petals and a fuzzy stem that grows two to three feet tall.

Black-eyed Susans grow in Chatham, New York, and elsewhere throughout the state.

JACK-IN-THE-PULPIT

One of the most **exotic**-looking plants in New York is the jack-in-the-pulpit. It is a common plant, with a green- or purple-striped spathe, or canopy, that hangs above the spadix, or spike, in its center. This looks like a preacher, or jack, in the pulpit—giving the plant its name. There are three varieties, which occupy high **elevations,** woodlands, and coastal areas.

A jack-in-the-pulpit plant can be one to three feet tall.

WILD ROSE

The wild roses of New York are pretty to look at, but should not be touched. Instead of just a few thorns, like flower-shop roses, these little beauties are covered with sharp spines. They grow best in swampy, wet soil—another reason why they should be viewed from afar! The rose is New York's state flower.

QUEEN ANNE'S LACE

The intricate white patterns formed by the flat blooms of Queen Anne's lace are hard to miss. This **species** grows in a variety of open spaces, from New York City to the Great Lakes. Technically, it is a wild carrot, but some people call it a bird's nest plant because its dried flower clusters curl up to form a small cup that looks like an abandoned nest. Many people think this plant smells faintly like carrots.

BEECH

The beech tree is instantly recognizable by its massive trunk and thin, blue-gray bark. The husk of the beech

Queen Anne's lace is a wildflower that blooms twice a year.

Growing Forests

Did you know that in 1890, only 20 percent of New York was covered by forest? Today, almost 62 percent of the state is covered by forest. What happened? Many people who had been farming the land decided to move to New York's cities; others found Midwest land that was better suited to farming. These areas that had formerly been farms gradually turned back into forest land. Also, New York's government realized that they wanted to protect their beautiful forests and spent time and money on **reforestation** efforts. During the **Great Depression** members of the **Civilian Conservation Corps** planted hundreds of thousands of trees across the state. This reforestation is an excellent example of how, with time and dedication, we can remake the world around us in a way that is healthy for everyone.

seed is covered with spikes—anyone running barefoot around a beech tree in the fall will remember not to do it again!

HEMLOCK

The hemlock tree grows well in cool, moist areas. Its most recognizable feature is its leaves: flat needles that are a shiny green on top and pale green with two white stripes on the bottom. The bark of older trees is a purplish brown and contains a high concentration of the chemical used to tan leather.

HICKORY

The straight trunk and narrow crown of the hickory make it easy to identify from a distance. Close up, you can tell a hickory by the shaggy strips of bark curling off it. This is believed to be a defense against squirrels that adore hickory nuts.

The sugar maple is the state tree of New York, Vermont, West Virginia, and Wisconsin. A red maple leaf also appears on Canada's flag.

OAK

There are several varieties of oak in New York state, including the white oak, red oak, and pin oak. The pin oak has made the most successful move from the forest to city streets. Its thin trunk and graceful, sweeping limbs make it the perfect shade tree for crowded city streets.

SUGAR MAPLE

In the fall, the sugar maple tree's seed pods helicopter down to the ground, and the leaves of the tree turn bright red and yellow. In late winter, when the temperatures at night drop to freezing levels and the days are warmed by the sun, a steady trickle of sap can be tapped from the sugar maple. This sap contains the sugar used to make maple syrup. The sugar maple can grow in almost any kind of soil, so it is found throughout the state. Before European settlers came to New York, Native Americans prized the sugar maple's hard wood for spearmaking. They taught settlers how to draw sap and make it into syrup—a process that was unknown to Europeans.

WHITE BIRCH

Besides being a beautiful tree, the white birch is also among the state's most useful. Settlers called it the canoe birch because its water-resistant outer skin could be stretched across a wooden frame to make a canoe. The white bark of the tree peels off the trunk easily in thin, paper-like strips. For this reason, it is sometimes called the paper birch, as well.

WHITE PINE

Of the many pine tree varieties in New York, the majestic white pine is the most common. It produces the white wood you see in the state's lumber yards,

The soft, white pine tree is often home to the caterpillars of one of New York's butterfly **species***: the eastern pine elfin. The caterpillars feed on the trees needles. This does not harm the tree in any way.*

which is used for everything from framing houses to basic carpentry. Its pinecones are long and slightly curved. The pinecones drop their seeds in the fall, then fall off themselves in the spring.

URBAN PLANTS

New York City's plants are famous for bringing color to the **urban** landscape. In city parks, window boxes, sidewalk planters, and hidden gardens grow hundreds of different **species,** some of which are quite spectacular. Still, the most amazing—and in many ways the most inspiring—are the tough little plants and trees that manage to grow within the concrete cracks and holes. They prove that beauty can exist in even the coldest and harshest environments.

• •

*Weeds are some of the most hearty and **adaptable** plants in the state of New York.. Their seeds are often distributed by the wind, so the plants often grow in unlikely places. They can even grow through cracks in an asphalt pavement in the middle of a city.*

A New York Food Web

In a food web, each level depends on the next. In New York, raccoons, ducks, and mice all eat acorns. Coyotes eat raccoons and ducks, and the lynx eats raccoons. If any plant or animal in the state were to become **endangered** or **extinct,** other members of the food chain would be affected.

Extinct Animals

When you hike through the forests and mountains of New York, you may be retracing the steps of long-**extinct** dinosaurs and early **mammals.** You may also be wandering through land that was once home to **species** that only recently vanished from the earth.

The evidence of dinosaur life in New York state comes from **fossil** footprints. Dino-prints can be seen mainly in two parts of the state: Long Island and Rockland County—which is just north and west of New York City.

The prints in Long Island belong to theropods, meat-eating three-toed dinosaurs that made these

One dinosaur that may have lived in Long Island is the three-toed, meat-eating Coelophysis.

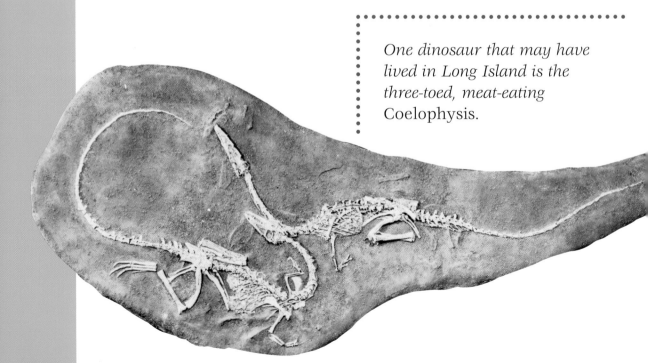

Old New York

What did New York look like when dinosaurs walked the Earth? The first thing you need to know is that New York was not where it is today. During the Triassic and Jurassic periods, the state was located very close to the **equator.** It was very hot, and sometimes very dry. At other times the land was very wet because it was close to an ancient ocean. New York was located where **continents** were pulling apart. Although there is no place on earth that compares to dinosaur-age New York, **archaeologists** think the closest match would be the region near Lake Tracona, in Africa.

impressions while wading through shallow water. They lived during the **Jurassic period,** 200 million years ago.

Rockland County has a greater variety of prints. They date from the late **Triassic period,** 220 million years ago. The prints belong to three basic groups of creatures: Artreipus, Grallator, and one that has yet to be classified.

There are other dino-prints in Rockland County, including ones belonging to a five-toed animal—possibly a member of the crocodile-like Rauisuschian family, the top **predators** of their time.

This fossil shows the footprints of a three-toed dinosaur, a line from its dragging tail, and ripples from shallow water.

PASSENGER PIGEON.

The last passenger pigeon died in 1914 at the Cincinnati Zoo.

After the dinosaurs died out, New York was home to a wide variety of early **mammals.** However, the **fossil** record does not tell a very good story. Most of what scientists know about New York's early mammals comes from knowledge of life forms that lived throughout this part of the **continent.** They are certain that mammoths and mastodons—prehistoric relatives of the elephant—and giant beavers lived in New York. They may have still been around when humans first reached the area over 10,000 years ago.

Passenger Pigeon

Not all **extinct** animals died out thousands of years ago. Two major bird extinctions occurred in New York as recently as the late 1800s. The passenger pigeon was once the most common bird in America. It moved in great flocks numbering in the many millions. The bird needed vast stretches of forest, which was being cleared at a fast pace. Also, it was extremely easy to catch. This combination of shrinking **habitat** and hungry humans wiped out the passenger pigeon flocks. By the time efforts started to save the **species,** it was too late.

Heath Hen

Hunting and habitat loss also doomed the heath hen, which was a common grassland bird when the first settlers came to Long Island. The heath hen nested on the ground in the tall grass and shrubs near the coast.

Contributing to the species' extinction was the introduction of cats to the **ecosystem,** as well as diseases spread by domestic chickens. The heath hen became extinct in New York state in 1932. People are now making efforts to protect New York's grassland habitats in order to prevent the loss of further animal or plant species.

The blue pike, shown here, became extinct in 1983 due to overfishing. Several varieties of another fish, called cisco, disappeared from Lake Erie because of pollution and hungry sea lampreys.

Foreign Invaders

Many invading plant and animal species have moved into New York from around the globe and have made it more difficult for **native** species to live in the area. If we are not careful, some of these invading species could push the native species to the point of extinction.

For example, sea lampreys—eel-like fish native to the Atlantic Ocean—have moved into the Great Lakes. Lampreys are **parasites**—they attach themselves to their prey to feed, as shown here. The number of lake trout in the Great Lakes has dropped significantly since lampreys found their way there in the 1930s.

Endangered Species

The wilderness and open land in New York state have allowed many plants and animals to live beside the state's 19 million human residents. However, there are places where the actions of humans have pushed **species** dangerously close to **extinction.** The state's **endangered** list includes **organisms** in every major plant and animal category. This chapter looks at one from each category, exploring the reasons why they are **threatened** and what their chances are of coming back.

••

*As developments spread into natural **habitats,** animals such as the black bear are found more frequently in New York state parks, alongside the human visitors.*

New York Wildlife Refuges

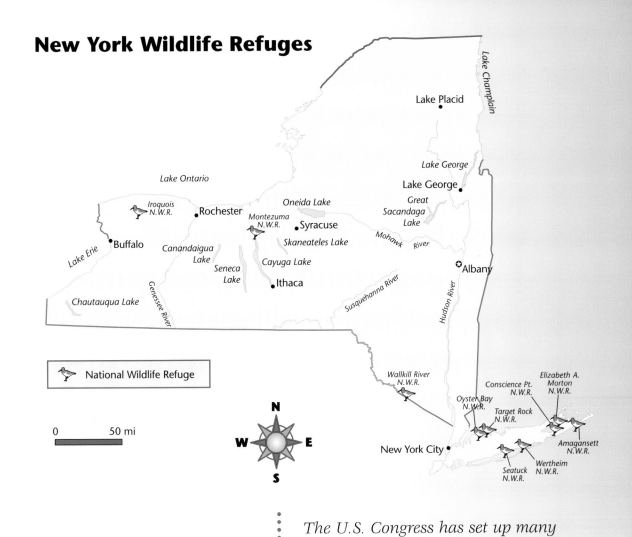

The U.S. Congress has set up many National Wildlife Refuges in New York. The U.S. Fish and Wildlife Service maintains them.

BOG TURTLE

There are 17 types of turtles that are **native** to New York state, including several ocean-going species. Three sea turtles—the leatherback, Atlantic ridley, and Atlantic hawksbill—are on the endangered list. The turtle New York scientists are most concerned about, however, is the bog turtle. At just over four inches long, it is the state's smallest turtle. It is possible to see it soaking up the sunshine in the spring, just after it emerges from **hibernation** in mid-April. You can tell a bog turtle by the bright yellow or orange splotch on each side of its head and neck.

The bog turtle lives in areas with shallow water, slow currents, dense mud, and plenty of light.

Bog turtle **habitats** do not make very good places to build houses. However, some housing developments are located close enough to wet areas so that turtles are caught by humans and kept as pets. This has contributed to their decline. The bog turtle's habitat is also **threatened** by tall plants such as reeds, which can invade these wet areas and then spread quickly. They block out the sun, which cools the ground temperature. This affects the bog turtle's eggs.

The news is not all bad for New York's bog turtle. During the last 25 years, scientists have studied the turtles closely. They have learned how to **breed** them in **captivity,** and soon babies may be set free in the wild. If its habitat is undisturbed by humans, a bog turtle may live more than 30 years.

PIPING PLOVER

Bird watchers along the beaches of Long Island eagerly await the arrival of the piping plover each March. Not only are they becoming a rare sight in New York, they also are usually the first shore birds to fly north for the **mating** season. The piping plover is five to six inches long, with an orange-and-black beak, black bands around its neck and forehead, and orange legs. The bird's feathers are the color of dry sand. This helps it **camouflage** itself on its nest, which is built on the open sand in beach areas.

As more people move to these areas, the piping plover's habitat has been disrupted. This is the second time in the last 100 years that its survival in New York has been threatened. The bird was hunted for meat and for sport until the Migratory Bird Treaty Act went into effect in 1918. The piping plover made a comeback in the 1920s, 1930s, and 1940s, but after World War II, when Long Island residents began to build lots of houses, the numbers began to decline again. The population has remained fairly steady in recent years because of state and federal wildlife protection laws. In some nesting areas, beaches are closed in the springtime.

Male and female piping plovers are very similar in size and in their coloring. All can be recognized by their sand-colored wing feathers, white underside, and orange legs.

STURGEON

One of New York's most **endangered** fish is the short-nose sturgeon, which spends its entire life in the Hudson River. It is this habitat which led to its decline, but also now holds great promise for its future. In the 1800s

The Atlantic sturgeon, like the shortnose sturgeon, is a victim of overfishing. Officials are now monitoring the populations of both kinds of sturgeon in the Hudson River.

and early 1900s, factories poured toxic waste into the river. The dumping reduced the oxygen in the water and killed off many fish.

This was just the beginning of the problems for the shortnose sturgeon. A bottom-feeder that feels around in the mud for food, it slurped up much of the pollution that settled in the depths of the river. At the same time, demand for sturgeon eggs and flesh was on the rise, and the shortnose was nearly fished out of existence.

What is known about sturgeon is fascinating. It is **anadromous,** which means it lives in salt water but lays its eggs in fresh water in the spring. Unlike most fish **species,** the shortnose sturgeon does not **spawn** every year. Males swim upriver to **mate** every other year, while females lay eggs every three years. Hatchlings are poor swimmers and tend to feed only along the bottom. If they make it to adulthood, however, they can live a very long time. One female is known to have reached her 67th birthday!

Without blue lupine, the Karner blue butterfly is a doomed species. And without Karner blues, many of the wildflowers they pollinate could suffer, too.

KARNER BLUE BUTTERFLY AND BLUE LUPINE

One of New York state's rarest and most spectacular butterflies is the Karner blue butterfly. With a wingspan of only an inch, the butterfly is not always easy to see, but the markings of its wings—deep violet-blue with white fringes—are not easily forgotten. The Karner blue's **larvae** get food from only one type of flower: the blue lupine. The female lays her eggs one at a time under its leaves or on its stem. As the blue lupine's **habitat** has shrunk, however, the butterfly population that feeds on it has declined, too.

*Blue lupine grows in the gently sloping, sandy **terrain** found in parts of the Hudson River valley.*

In centuries past, when trees burned after lightning strikes, the blue lupine filled the gaps quickly. In recent years, however, this habitat has come under great pressure for two reasons. First, the river views from these areas make them popular building sites. Second, fire prevention has kept the oak and pine from burning off, which has limited the places where lupine can exist.

SNAKES

New York is not really known for its reptiles, but there are more than 20 different **species** of lizards and snakes. Two snakes, the Eastern hognose and worm snake, appear to be shrinking in number. A third, the timber rattlesnake, is considered **threatened,** while a fourth—the Eastern massasauga—is on the **endangered** list for the state of New York.

The massasauga rattlesnake is smaller than the timber rattlesnake, and is known as the "swamp rattler." It prefers wetland **habitats** such as riverbottoms and marshes, and it feeds on small **rodents,** frogs, and birds. If undisturbed by humans, a massasauga can live up to 14 years.

TIGER SALAMANDER

The Eastern tiger salamander, one of the largest salamanders in the United States, has become endangered in the state of New York. This spotted **amphibian** spends most of its time underground, so it is considered a "mole salamander." It most often will live in a pine **barren** area near a pond, where it can **breed.** Construction and recreational off-roading are a

*Eastern tiger salamanders can grow to be 10 inches long and reach 15 years of age. Their **predators** include fish, snakes, and birds.*

Only in One Place

The Chittenango ovate amber snail lives in only one place in the entire world: near a 100-foot-high waterfall in New York. It is considered an endangered species because of its limited habitat and because, since its discovery in 1905, its numbers seem to have steadily decreased. By the 1990s, there were fewer than 25 of the snail in existence. Efforts are now in place to maintain the snail's population by raising some in **captivity** as well as protecting them in their natural habitat. The waterfall in which the Chittenango snail live is within Chittenango State Park. Visitors to the park are not allowed near the waterfall or its surrounding plants and rocks where the snails live, because if the habitat were to become polluted, this species might be lost.

constant threat to the breeding sites and general habitat and **migration** patterns. In New York, the tiger salamander is found only on Long Island.

NORTHERN CRICKET FROG

Another endangered species in New York is a tiny tree frog. The northern cricket frog is an amazing creature, able to leap five to six feet despite being only one inch long! The frog was named for its breeding call, which sounds much like a cricket's chirp. Much of the frog's population has died out due to human pollution of its natural habitat. The decline can be traced to the 1950s and 1960s in particular, when people were spraying DDT and other **pesticides** over ponds and wetland areas in the state. Today, few northern cricket frogs can be found in the state other than a few scattered populations in the Hudson Highlands.

Endangered and Threatened Species

The New York State Department of Environmental Conservation monitors animals and plants that are **threatened** or **endangered** in the state. A **species** often is added to the list when the environment of the plant or animal has been altered in some way, such as by disease, natural occurrences, or overcollection by humans. Those listed as being of special concern are not yet threatened, but show signs that they may become endangered if factors do not change.

Endangered in New York

Allegheny woodrat
American burying beetle
Atlantic hawksbill sea turtle
Atlantic ridley sea turtle
Blue whale
Bog turtle
Chittenango ovate amber snail
Cougar
Dwarf wedgemussel
Eskimo curlew
Golden eagle
Gray wolf
Grizzled skipper
Humpback whale
Indiana bat
Karner blue butterfly
Leatherback sea turtle
Massasauga
Mud turtle
Northern cricket frog
Peregrine falcon
Pink mucket
Piping plover
Pugnose shiner
Queen snake
Right whale
Roseate tern
Short-eared owl
Shortnose sturgeon
Sperm whale
Spruce grouse
Tiger salamander

Threatened in New York

Bald eagle
Canada lynx
Common tern
Frosted elfin
Gravel chub
Green sea turtle
Lake sturgeon
Least bittern
Loggerhead sea turtle
Mud sunfish
Northeastern beach tiger beetle
Sedge wren
Swamp darter
Timber rattlesnake

Special Concern in New York

Buffalo pebble snail
Common loon
Common sanddragon
Eastern box turtle
Harbor porpoise
Hellbender
Marbled salamander
Mountain brook lamprey
New England cottontail
Pygmy snaketail
Red-headed woodpecker
Red-shouldered hawk
Small-footed bat
Southern leopard frog
Spotted turtle

People, Plants, and Animals

When **habitats** are altered by humans, some species are driven away, while others **adapt** and survive. The most dramatic changes come when cities rise where open land had existed for countless centuries. Creatures must find new **niches,** change old behaviors, and learn how to live with humans. Of the many animals that have adapted to city living, none have adapted as well as the squirrel and the pigeon.

Away from New York's cities and into its wilderness areas, **reintroduction** is the big success story. Several species that had almost disappeared from the state have made great comebacks thanks to the efforts of people concerned with the preservation of New York's **ecosystems.**

This gray squirrel is making its way across the fire escape of a New York City building.

Feeding Squirrels

The food most often fed to squirrels in big city parks is peanuts. However, peanuts may not be good for them. Some scientists believe that fur loss and poor eyesight are due to too many peanuts in the squirrel's diet.

GRAY SQUIRREL

The most familiar **urban mammal** in New York is the eastern gray squirrel. The city squirrel is fearless and friendly because it depends on people for most of its food. It lives in parks, rarely going beyond the entrances.

In the woods, squirrels are active in the early morning and evening, when there is less light and it is easier to blend in with the surroundings. They eat acorns of the white oak, and hickory and hazel nuts.

Gray squirrels have also **adapted** well to city life. In city parks, squirrels will approach people who are eating food. They will stuff themselves on whatever people feed them, throw in garbage cans, or drop on the ground. Park squirrels have adjusted their schedules for greatest contact with humans, who visit the park in greatest numbers from mid-morning to afternoon.

ROCK DOVE

The pigeon familiar to New Yorkers is actually a rock dove. This blue-gray bird is called a rock dove because it nests on rocky ledges. New York's cities have millions of stone ledges, and thus there are millions of these birds in the state. They build flimsy nests of twigs and grass, and typically raise one or two chicks at a time. Five weeks after they hatch, the chicks are ready to fly.

The city pigeon has other talents. It happens to be one of the fastest-flying birds in North America, yet it can change speed and direction in a flash. And if it can avoid cars, trucks, cats, and **birds of prey,** it will live 10 to 15 years.

Rock doves can be found in great numbers in New York's city parks and streets.

Although the rock dove has made itself at home in New York, it is not a **native** bird. It was brought to North America by Europeans in the 1500s and 1600s. Many of the state's animals and plants came from other places. Sometimes they blend right in, without changing the balance of nature. However, these **invaders** often crowd out native **species.**

HOUSE SPARROW

A common bird from Europe to Africa and southern Asia, the house sparrow was brought to New York City in the 1850s. Within 50 years it was one of the most common birds in the United States. House sparrows built their nests one next to the other. They liked barns and stables, where hundreds of nests could be squeezed together along the support beams. Birds that had previously nested in these spots were overwhelmed and driven from the city.

The German cockroach is not a very welcome member of New York's wildlife, but it shows no signs of disappearing.

Today, you almost never see a house sparrow in New York City. When the automobile replaced the horse as a means of transportation, the city's stables were converted into living space for humans. Its **habitat** destroyed, the house sparrow moved out into the country, where it is now doing just fine.

Cockroach

One **invader** that has not been crowded out is the cockroach. Most of the world's 6,000 cockroach **species** live in the wild, under dead bark or in rotting vegetation. In New York's cities, however, the German cockroach has made itself right at home among humans.

Cockroaches have long been hated by New Yorkers. The dirty insects are never a welcome visitor in any home or business. Yet for many years they were tolerated as part of city life. They were said to eat bed bugs, which is true, and also that they did not spread or cause diseases, which may not be true. Recent links between roach droppings and childhood asthma suggest that roaches may be affecting the health of city children.

Peregrine Falcon

A more inspiring story of **urban** success is that of the peregrine falcon. Along with the raven and osprey, it is one of the world's widest-ranging birds, so the fact that it has found a home among the skyscrapers, bridges, and water towers of New York should not be a surprise.

Still, when New Yorkers catch a glimpse of one these birds streaking across the skyline, they tend to be amazed.

The peregrine has made a home on every **continent** but Antarctica, yet only in North America was it **threatened** with **extinction.** Use of **pesticides** and loss of habitat threatened this beautiful bird, but thanks to greater environmental awareness and a successful **breeding** program, the peregrine has made a comeback.

Normally, peregrines feed on **waterfowl.** But in New York City they feast on pigeons. Peregrines are one of the few **birds of prey** that can catch the sneaky creatures because they actually fly the same way. Often what New Yorkers think are pigeons darting between the buildings are peregrines in pursuit of a meal.

ZEBRA MUSSEL

One species that New Yorkers aren't as eager to protect is the zebra mussel. These **mollusks** can be recognized by their zebra-like, black-and-white stripes. Adults grow

This family of peregrine falcons is nesting on the Brooklyn Bridge. Peregrine falcons can be found in many unlikely places throughout New York City.

Zebra mussels were brought to New York unintentionally from Europe in the late 1980s and have been a nuisance ever since.

to be about two inches long. They attach themselves to solid objects in fresh or slightly salty water. The zebra mussel's oval-shaped shell can easily block water pipes. They also stick to boat hulls and damage engine-cooling systems. Furthermore, as with any invasive **species,** zebra mussels pose a threat to the balance of other plant and animal species in New York's rivers and lakes.

The Big Clean Up

Many more species would be **endangered** or **extinct** were it not for the Clean Water Act of 1972. The federal government passed laws forcing cities and towns to treat their sewage before releasing it into the environment, and required factories to obtain permits before releasing chemicals into surrounding waters. The strict regulations greatly affected New York, which had some of the most polluted waters in North America. Since 1972, several **threatened** species of fish and birds have recovered. Many others have returned or have been successfully **reintroduced** to habitats that were once too polluted for them to survive.

Another problem that is being addressed is runoff from storm drains. In places where roads have been built near tidal wetlands—particularly on Long Island—harmful pollutants, such as the road salt used in ice removal, wash into the **ecosystem.** These waters are home to the tiny creatures at the beginning of the food chain. If they are destroyed, the effects would be devastating. The Fresh Water Wetlands Act came into effect several years ago to limit development and protect these sensitive areas.

The bald eagle has made a comeback in New York thanks to the efforts of concerned citizens.

BALD EAGLES

In recent years, New Yorkers have been shocked to see bald eagles in the skies. The decline of this bird in North America during the 20th century led to a new awareness about the terrible effects of pollution on all **birds of prey.** Studies found that there were **pesticides** in the brain and eggs of the bald eagle. After waters of New York state were cleaned up in the 1980s, and the fish bald eagles eat were healthy, the bald eagle was reintroduced. In the 1990s, several birds were set free in New York, and their numbers have grown even faster than people had hoped.

WILD TURKEY

The wild turkey has made an even bigger comeback. Once hunted out of existence in New York state, it is now strong again. The wild turkey was successfully reintroduced during the 1960s, and its numbers have increased so much in recent years that it can now be legally hunted in many parts of the state.

*These two male wild turkeys are showing their tail feathers to the females in their group, hoping to find a **mate.** This mating behavior takes place in early spring.*

LYNX

The lynx, a relative of the bobcat, is also being **reintroduced.** This **species,** built for cold weather, had disappeared from New York state in the late 1800s. The bobcat, more suited to a warmer **climate,** proved to be more **adaptable** to the changes brought about by humans. Scientists have learned much about the lynx from studies in Canada since then, and now believe it can live successfully in the northern part of New York.

LOOKING TO THE FUTURE

The plants and animals of New York are a truly spectacular group—from the tiniest frog to the massive moose, from the dandelion to the sugar maple. It is our duty to protect New York's wildlife and make certain that it survives long into the future.

Some lynx from Canada have been brought to upstate New York in hopes of restoring the population once found there.

Map of New York

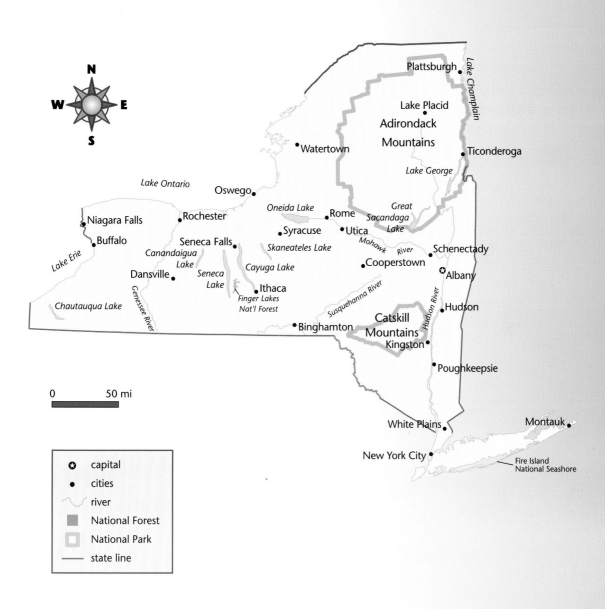

N
W E
S

Plattsburgh
Lake Champlain
Lake Placid
Adirondack
Mountains
• Watertown
Ticonderoga
Lake George

Lake Ontario
Oswego
Great
Sacandaga
Lake
Oneida Lake
Rome
Niagara Falls
Rochester
Syracuse
Utica
Buffalo
Seneca Falls
Mohawk River
Schenectady
Lake Erie
Canandaigua
Lake
Skaneateles Lake
Cooperstown
Dansville
Seneca
Lake
Cayuga Lake
Albany
Genessee River
Ithaca
Finger Lakes
Nat'l Forest
Susquehanna River
Hudson
Hudson River
Chautauqua Lake
Binghamton
Catskill
Mountains
Kingston
Poughkeepsie

0   50 mi

White Plains
Montauk
New York City
Fire Island
National Seashore

✪	capital
•	cities
∿	river
■	National Forest
▢	National Park
—	state line

CANADA
Maine
Vermont
New
Hampshire
New York
Massachusetts
Rhode Island
Connecticut
Ohio
Pennsylvania
Atlantic
Ocean
New
Jersey

Glossary

adapt   make suitable or able to function

amphibian   animal that lives in and around both water and land

anadromous   running upward

archaeologist   person who studies history through the things that people have made or built

barren   area of flat land with limited vegetation

biodiversity   biological variety in an environment as shown by the number of different kinds of plants and animals

birds of prey   birds that feed almost entirely on meat taken from hunting

breed   to produce offspring

brush   heavy growth of bushes and small trees

camouflage   blending in with surroundings to hide

captivity   under control of humans, often in a zoo

Civilian Conservation Corps   public works program that gave over three million young men and adults work during the Great Depression in the United States

climate   weather conditions that are usual for a certain area

continent   one of the great divisions of land on the globe; Asia, Antarctica, Australia, Africa, Europe, North America, and South America are the seven continents of the world

dam   barrier to hold back a flow of water

dominance   control over others

ecosystem   community of living things, together with the environment in which they live

edible   safe to eat

elevation   height, especially above sea level

endangered   at risk of dying out

equator   imaginary circle around Earth at an equal distance from the North and South poles

estuary   arm of the sea at the lower end of a river

exotic   introduced from a foreign country

extinct   no longer living

fell   to cut or knock down

fossil   remains of prehistoric plants or animals that have turned to stone

graze   feed on grass and other plants that grow close to the ground

Great Depression   economic collapse in 1929, in which unemployment was high and many businesses failed

habitat   place where an animal or plant lives

hardy   able to withstand harsh conditions or severe weather

hibernation   to pass through the winter in a resting state

inland   not near the seacoast

insulating   keeps something warm

invader   something that enters by force and does not belong there

Jurassic period   time of the Mesozoic era between the Triassic and Cretaceous, marked by the presence of dinosaurs and the first birds

larvae   wingless form in which many insects are born

mammal   warm-blooded animal with a backbone; female mammals produce milk for feeding their young

mate   breeding partner

migrate   to move from one place to another for food or to breed

mollusk   animal that lives in a shell

native   originally from a certain area

niche   place that is best suited for something or someone

nocturnal   active at night

organism   living person, animal, or plant

parasite   plant or animal that lives in or on some other living thing and gets food and shelter from it

pesticide   substance used to destroy pests

plumage   feathers of a bird

predator   animal that lives mostly by killing and eating other animals

prong   slender part that sticks out, like as a point on an antler

reforestation   to renew forest growth by planting new trees

reintroduce   bring something back to a place where it once was

rodent   any of a group of mammals (such as squirrels, mice, and rats) with sharp front teeth used for gnawing

spawn   produce or deposit eggs

species   group of plants or animals that look and behave the same way

terrain   features of the surface of a piece of land

threatened   group of animals whose numbers are decreasing, bringing the group close to endangerment

Triassic period   earliest part of the Mesozoic era, marked by the appearance of dinosaurs

urban   relating to the city

waterfowl   bird found in or near water

More Books to Read

Ball, Jacqueline, et. al. *New York.* Cleveland, Ohio: World Almanac Education, 2002.

Cotter, Kristin. *New York.* Danbury, Conn.: Children's Press, 2002.

Heinrichs, Ann, et. al. *New York.* Danbury, Conn.: Children's Press, 1999.

MacMillian, Dianne M. *Life in a Deciduous Forest.* Minneapolis: Lerner Publications, 2003.

Spilsbury, Richard and Louise. *Plant Habitats.* Chicago: Heinemann Library, 2002.

Index

About the Author

Mark Stewart was born and raised in New York City. He now lives across the water in New Jersey, where his office overlooks the metropolitan skyline. A graduate of Duke University with a degree in history, Stewart has authored more than 100 nonfiction titles for the school and library market. He and his wife Sarah have two daughters, Mariah and Rachel.